prayer

A Highly Favoured Life Devotional

Copyright © The Highly Favoured Life 2022

Published and Designed by Unmovable Publications

ALL RIGHTS RESERVED to The Highly Favoured Life and authorized writers.

No part of this book may be reproduced, transmitted, or sold in any form or by any means, electronic, or mechanical, including photocopying, recording, or by any information storage and retrieval system, without permission in writing from the publisher.

All scripture quotations are from the King James Version (KJV) of the Bible.

1st Edition published in 2022
2nd Edition published in 2025

ISBN:
978-1-967189-04-5 (paperback)
978-1-967189-05-2 (hardback)

Table of Contents

One Thing Is Needful - Time with my God 9
   By Lydia L. Riley

Praying For A Need 13
   By Andrea Leeder

Prayer of the Heart 17
   By Sharon Garrett

God-Prompted Prayer 21
   By Renee Patton

Peaceful Pause in Prayer 25
   By Kathy Lane

Prayer Is Essential 31
   By Jenny Young

Prayer Is All We Need 35
   By Marsha Leto

A Little Talk with Jesus 39
   By Angie Marco

Prayer Changes...Me!. 43
   By Kim Thompson

Praying for Her 47
   By Nicole Redmon

Powerful Prayer 51
   By Julie Payne

Prayer for the Weary Mama 55
   By Courtney Womack

In His Time. 59
   Anonymous

How Could I Pray For Hurtful People? 63
   By Larissa Bell

We Ought Always To Pray 69
   By Debra Birner

Always to Pray 73
   By Kaylena Cinereski

Teach Us To Pray 77
   By Elizabeth J. Garrett

P-R-A-Y-E-R 81
   By Kelly Byrley

Paying the Price of Prayer 87
   By Misty Wells

Abiding in Prayer 91
   By Coretta Gomes

Praying for Your Friends 95
   By Callie Payne

The Hour of Prayer 99
   By Dixie Sasser

Faithful in Prayer 103
   By Corli Hall

First Things First 109
   By Alyssa Schutt

The Direct Approach 113
   By Marissa Patton

Promptly Pray! 117
   By Janette Young

A Testimony of Prayer 123
   By Ruth Weaver

Getting God's Attention Through Prayer . . . 127
   By Nicky Schutt

Call on The Name of The Lord 131
   By Kate Ledbetter

Is Sin Keeping You from Prayer? 135
   By Grace Shiflett

Teach Me to Pray 139
   By Rikki Beth Poindexter

Dedication

To Janette Young, thank you for showing us by example your relationship with God. Thank you for being a praying wife, mother, grandmama, and great-grandmama. We love you!

To these writers who have set an example of prayer, thank you for teaching us to pray! Your fellowship with the Father is an inspiration.

Introduction

One Thing Is Needful
By Lydia L. Riley

The "one thing" my heart does seek,
The "one thing" I desire;
To dwell in Your presence, Lord,
And linger awhile.
Endless tasks may be pressing me.
Heavy burdens oppressing me,
But I need to stop and sit down at Your feet.

I gaze back upon my day,
As evening falls around,
And often gauge my love for You
As I look around,
Showing You the list of things I've done,
Pointing out the race I've tried to run,
But You gently speak to me this simple truth:

Yes, there's those who've need of me,
I've got a lot to do,
But there is a balance, Lord,
And I need time with You.
To show how much You mean to me,
My heart listening, Your Truths to see.
Time with You my God is not a wasted thing.

One thing is needful;
One thing is key:
To spend time with my God,
Just listening at His feet.

Nothing too urgent to keep me away;
My Jesus wants some time with me today.
This one thing,
This "good part,"
I will give You from my heart.

Others may be busy
While I stop and pray.
"This is such a waste of time,"
I can almost hear them say.
My efforts may be scattered,
My talents may be few,
But this is one thing I can surely do!

One thing is needful;
One thing is key:
To spend time with my God,
Just listening at His feet.
Nothing too urgent to keep me away;
My Jesus wants some time with me today.
This one thing,
This good part,
I will give Him this one thing!

This beautiful song was written by one of our authors, Lydia L. Riley. It is taken from the passage of Scripture in Luke 10:38-42. The music can be found on her website: seasonsoflifepublications.com.

One Thing Is Needful - Time with my God

By Lydia L. Riley

But one thing is needful: and Mary hath chosen that good part, which shall not be taken away from her.

Luke 10:42

As a Christian, there are special times in our lives when one message completely changes us, where God shows us things and teaches us lessons we will never get over. Such is the case with a message my pastor preached last summer – it was his final point and the Lord got ahold of my heart with a message that will not let me go. I've been saved for over forty years, and this simple thought has forever changed me. The story is so very familiar, from a passage I have cherished and heard throughout my life as a believer, and yet somehow the Lord worked such a powerful and divine way within my heart.

In Luke's account, we have the story of Mary – the one who loved Jesus with every fiber of her being. Her sister Martha is busy serving, also a necessary act and a way of showing her love to the Savior. Yet, when Martha tries to get their Lord to reprimand her sister, Jesus states something so simple, and yet so profound – "one thing is needful: and Mary hath chosen that good part, which shall not be taken away from her."

Jesus knew that he was soon to go to Calvary. He yearned for someone to sit and listen to Him, for someone to just take the time to be with Him during His final hours on this earth. Someone to just be there for Him, a friend that would just spend time with Him and listen. Mary was the only one who seemed to be in tune with these deep emotions, choosing to stop everything in her life and just sit at His feet and hear His Word. Jesus refused to take this "good thing" away from her and commended her with His words of love and approval. Of all the things that we can do and say and be for the Lord, this is the one thing that Jesus chooses to state is needful – absolutely essential, even if everything else is to be left undone. The one thing that is truly important when we get to the end of our day, and even to the end of our lives – the one thing that Jesus says will really matter – the time spent with our Lord.

"How often do we end up being so busy "doing things" to show our love for God, but don't spend time with Him? Yes, we need to be busy showing mercy, and loving our neighbor, but we can't get so busy that we neglect to spend time with the Lord. Urgent things tend to get in the way of important things. We can get so busy working that we become distracted to the one thing that is truly needed. Jesus wants someone to listen to Him. The Lord wants someone to talk to. There is balance in the Christian life. To sit and spend time with God is not wasted time; this is the needful thing." (Quotations are taken from my personal sermon notes from my pastor.)

The Psalmist also states a similar thought when he declares "One thing have I desired of the LORD ..." – dwelling in His presence, beholding His beauty, enquiring in His temple. David also knew the great value of this "One Thing" – spending time with God! (Ps. 27:4)

prayer

Date: /   /   Scripture:

Notes:

Requests:

Blessings:

Praying For A Need

By Andrea Leeder

Be careful for nothing; but in every thing by prayer and supplication with thanksgiving let your requests be made known unto God.

Philippians 4:6

I believe one of the most important things in our Christian life is praying. God said, in everything by prayer and supplication. He wants us to pray about everything. How many times do we make a decision without ever asking God about it? We have already made our minds up about something and we never even bothered to ask God if that is what He wanted us to do. If we pray about questionable situations that come into our lives, God will give us answers. We will make better decisions if we pray and ask God to help us before we make a decision. God hears the prayers of those little things that do not mean much to others, but mean something to you.

When I was young, I had really crooked teeth. As a teenager, I prayed and prayed for braces. To most people, that seems silly, but it was something important to me, at the time. We were missionaries on the mission field, and there were five kids in my family. I was not the only one of my siblings who needed braces, but God made a way for me to get them. I knew God did that just for me! He answered my prayer! That was one of the first prayers I really remember God answering just for me. I still think about that answer to prayer. I am reminded that God cares and hears even the smallest of prayers.

Prayer is a way to build a relationship with God. He wants to hear our thoughts and burdens. The times when we feel we can talk to no one about a need, we can talk to God. When we feel all alone, go to Him in prayer. God gives us a comfort that no one on earth can give. He can give us peace that passeth all understanding. In the midst of a storm in your life, God can give a peace and comfort that only He can give. God tells us to pray without ceasing. When hope seems lost, pray! When life is good, pray! When there are decisions that need to be made, pray! It does not matter our situation, we need to pray!

Challenge yourself. The next time a need arises, go to God in prayer. Whether it is a need for someone else or yourself personally. Whatever it may be, go to God first!

prayer

Date: / /   Scripture:

Notes:

Requests:

Blessings:

Prayer of the Heart

By Sharon Garrett

...but the Spirit itself maketh intercession for us with groanings which cannot be uttered.

Romans 8:26b

When we think of prayer, we think of words: talking to communicate. As I look more deeply, I realize that communication is not always spoken words. I remembered the hug, tears, and hand clasp when I greeted a recently-widowed friend. The communication that passed between us was too deep for spoken words. Heart communed with heart because we felt the same grief. I too was widowed a few years ago. Her grief was more recent, but it was a mutual understanding that passed between us.

As I looked in the Holy Scriptures, I found some "nuggets" concerning heart communication with God. Sometimes the heart is so overwhelmed with a need to hear from heaven that our heart groans within us. Romans 8:26b, "...but the Spirit itself maketh intercession for us with groanings which cannot be uttered." To me, prayer is a pouring out of the heart to God with the assurance that the Holy Spirit in us is communing with God. Psalm 142:2, "I poured out my complaint before him; I shewed before him my trouble." It is a longing for God-a longing for His presence, whether the burden or pain is a personal need or a need for someone else. Psalm 62:8a, "Trust in the him at all times; ye people, pour out your heart before him...." Psalm 55:4a says, "My heart is sore pained within me...."

There are times when we have public prayers, and of course, they are spoken words. But during our private prayer, there is a longing of the soul that is too deep to be expressed with words. Psalm 84:2, "My soul longeth yea, even fainteth for the courts of the Lord; my heart and my flesh crieth out for the living God."

We all need these times when our heart and soul are pained within us, and the longing to hear from our heavenly Father is so great that it compels us to groan within our being for Him. There always follows a sweet peace. We may not receive the request that drew us to that place, but when we pour out our hearts before Him there is an unspeakable peace. Do you need peace about a problem or situation for which you do not have an answer? Find that secret place and just pour out your heart before Him. He will meet you in that secret place of prayer.

prayer

Date: /   /   Scripture:

Notes:

Requests:

Blessings:

God-Prompted Prayer

By Renee Patton

Trust in him at all times; ye people, pour out your heart before him: God is a refuge for us. Selah.

Psalm 62:8

How often do we feel God prick our heart with someone's name or a need one has? Do we STOP to PRAY when prompted by God? Well, I have learned to be soft towards the Lord's prompting!

Many years ago during a camp meeting, a preacher recounted an instance when God prompted him to pray for his son. The preacher told how his son worked with his hands and did physical labor. One evening while his son was at work, the preacher was changing a ceiling fan in his living room. While on the ladder he felt God pricking his heart to pray for his son. The preacher tried to resist. Then God pricked his heart even harder. The preacher wanted to finish the job of changing the ceiling fan, continuing to resist.

Isn't this true of many of us? When we start something, we do not care to be interrupted until the task is complete!

Well, God pricked his heart again! Finally, the preacher gave into the Lord and climbed down off the ladder and prayed for his son! The preacher happened to note the time vas he knelt to pray. The preacher recounted as he prayed that God must have had good reason to intercede with the task. He then poured out his heart to the Lord and asked for guidance and protection of his son. When finished praying, the preacher climbed up the ladder to finish the task. Then after completion, he began descending the ladder and his son walked through the door. The son walks in bloody and with bandages and tells him of the terrible accident he was in at work and how much worse it could have been; however, at the same time noted as when the preacher began praying, the son said it was like a miracle, the problem ceased, and he was not further injured. I do remember the preacher saying his son very well could have been killed, but God intervened.

That story has stuck with me over the last 26 years. When I feel God's prompting on my heart for someone, I try to STOP and PRAY right then!

Recently, my daughter was pregnant with her second child, and God prompted my heart to pray for her. She has had many complications from auto-immune issues and her first pregnancy was physically difficult for her. I did not know why God so deeply impressed on my heart to pray, but pray I did! For seven months I prayed! I had this message of the preacher come to mind many times and asked God for guidance and protection in her life, especially because of this continual prompting. I pray for all my children and grandchildren, but this was just a bit different. I'll never know if God spared her and her son because of this prompting, but I do know things were not worse for her because I did STOP and PRAY when God prompted my heart! Trust Him and pour out your heart! God does hear us when we pray!

Do you STOP and PRAY when God prompts your heart?

prayer

Date: /   /   Scripture:

Notes:

Requests:

Blessings:

Peaceful Pause in Prayer

By Kathy Lane

---

*Be still, and know that I am God: I will be exalted among the heathen,
I will be exalted in the earth.*

Psalm 46:10

My personality is very administrative by nature. I love planning, organizing, distributing tasks, and so on. When the Lord blessed our family with a side business, I immensely enjoyed learning all the aspects of running a business from accounting, the employees, and the customers. As God continued to bless our business, it was becoming harder to find the time to keep up with the demands, as my husband and I were both on full time staff at our church as well.

Year after year, both the business and church ministries continued to flourish. We were very busy as we tried constantly to prioritize family, ministry, work, and our business. Long 16-hour days were not uncommon for us. Though it definitely was not easy, we felt privileged that God had blessed our family with these wonderful open doors to work hard and be a part of some amazing opportunities.

"Be still, and know that I am God: I will be exalted among the heathen, I will be exalted in the earth."

- Psalm 46:10

Now, I must admit, there were times when I would be so busy administrating that my husband, in his wisdom, would pull me away from it all. He would remind me that I needed to "stop and sharpen the ax." He knew that I needed to take time to step back, reevaluate, and confirm we were still going in the right direction, and that made me think about the spiritual "pauses" in my life. As much as I enjoy staying busy and taking advantage of all the time-saving advancements in technology, I would still be wise to cautiously approach how it may be influencing my daily life.

We have been inundated with everything today being instant. That philosophy of instant fulfillment can inadvertently spill over into our spiritual lives and become detrimental to our walk. We no longer know how to be still, to be quiet, to meditate, to listen – because we're simply too busy moving on to the next thing. Our lives have become so cluttered with the "noise" of our current culture that we do not know how to "pause," causing our minds to constantly wander. Becoming antsy, we immediately turn to our phones to drown out the silence. We have been conditioned with the NOW philosophy – we want internet service now; we want packages now; and heaven forbid we wait longer than fifteen minutes at a restaurant for our food because we have things to do and our time is valuable! (But more valuable than souls?)

So, would it be correct to speculate that if we are so impatient physically, that we may be unintentionally putting expectations on

God spiritually? Do we put the Lord on a time schedule regarding our prayers being answered? Are we spending more time in prayer asking instead of listening? Prayer is not single-faceted; it is not only about communicating our burdens and petitions before the Lord (though in Psalms 55:22 and Phil. 4:6 it clearly states that we ought to do so) – but there is another aspect of prayer that we often overlook. It is the peaceful pause in prayer.

This is where we stop talking and do not say one word. Instead, in quietness, we listen for His still, small voice. I believe that God is continuing to call more believers into His service; however, since many have allowed the noise and ideologies of this world to overpower the voice of God, they simply cannot hear Him. Is our spiritual ax becoming dull because we have not learned the spiritual discipline of cultivated "silence" in our prayer time? We must purposefully pull away from all the daily distractions and pause long enough to hear the voice of the Lord speaking in silent prayer. "Be still and know that I am God…" Let us not be guilty of allowing distractions and the ceaseless noise of this world to drown out the still small voice of our Heavenly Father.

"A closed mouth before God and a silent heart are indispensable for the reception of certain kinds of truth. No man is qualified to speak who has not first listened." A.W. Tozer

prayer

Date: / /   Scripture:

Notes:

Requests:

Blessings:

Prayer Is Essential

By Jenny Young

Let us therefore come boldly unto the throne of grace, that we may obtain mercy, and find grace to help in time of need.

Hebrews 4:16

Every Christian at some point in their life has struggled with having a daily, consistent prayer life. Why? Because our flesh and the devil does not want us to pray. The flesh wants us to get that extra hour of sleep, or keep playing that game, or keep talking to that friend. Our flesh is weak and has no desire to do anything spiritual. That is why we must die daily to our fleshly desires and wants. If we feed the flesh, the flesh will win every time.

The devil doesn't want us to pray either, because he knows that is where we get our help, strength, and encouragement to live for God every day of our lives. The devil will throw every kind of distraction or excuse our way to keep us from praying. We must not let the devil defeat our prayer life and take away our relationship with God. If the devil stops us from praying, he stops our spiritual growth in the Lord.

Prayer should be as important to us as breathing. Just as we cannot live physically without breath, we cannot live the Christian life without prayer. If we are going to do anything for God or be the Christian and example that God wants us to be, we must spend time in prayer.

We need to ask God daily to help us fight our flesh and to fight the devil. If we ask God for help, He is going to come running to help us. He will hear the cry of His child. He cannot ignore our requests if we are right with Him. I John 5:14 says: "And this is the confidence that we have in him, that, if we ask any thing according to his will, he heareth us:"

prayer

Date: / /   Scripture:

Notes:

Requests:

Blessings:

Prayer Is All We Need

By Marsha Leto

Be careful for nothing; but in every thing by prayer and supplication with thanksgiving let your requests be known unto God. And the peace of God, which passeth all understanding, shall keep your hearts and minds through Christ Jesus.

Philippians 4:6-7

Someone once said, "Prayer is the greatest tool we have against the devil." What a powerful statement that is! When the struggles of life come, we have to remind ourselves that we have all we need to live the victorious Christian life.

In I Chronicles 16:11, we read "Seek the Lord and his strength, seek his face continually." I love that Jesus never tires of hearing us pray. Isn't it wonderful that the Lord is not like the teacher or mom that threatens to change her name because she hears it so many times?

I don't know about you, but there have been times in the last year I have struggled with being anxious. I am so glad that 1 Peter 5:7 is in the Bible – "Casting all your care upon him; for he careth for you." He did not make us hold on to our problems, but rather to give them to Him. There have been so many times in my own life that the Lord took the heavy burden from me and replaced it with joy and peace.

There is such a great peace in giving the Lord our cares of life. When I do that, I am saying "Lord, I trust You and the way You are going to answer this problem." Romans 8:28 "And we know all things work together for good to them that love God, to them who are the called according to his purpose." Christ knows what is best for us, even better than what we think is best.

Lastly, I will praise Him for answered prayer. I love telling the Lord how great He is and thanking Him for all He has done! Hebrews 13:15-16 says, "By him therefore let us offer the sacrifice of praise to God continually, that is, the fruit of our lips giving thanks to his name. But to do good and to communicate forget not: for with such sacrifices God is well pleased." I am encouraged when I praise the Lord for the specific prayers answered.

Idea – Start a prayer journal for answered prayer. This has increased my faith. When I look over the prayers, I think God did it then and He will do it again.

What problem can you give to the Lord today?

prayer

Date: / /   Scripture:

Notes:

Requests:

Blessings:

A Little Talk with Jesus

By Angie Marco

Thou wilt keep him in perfect peace, whose mind is stayed on thee: because he trusteth in thee.

Isaiah 26:3

I took a deep breath as my husband and I opened up and read my CT scan results. Everything came back normal! How is it possible? Was this all a mistake in the first place? I had been diagnosed with pulmonary fibrosis six weeks before this day.

We were finally done going back and forth to doctor's offices, and labs for blood work, X-rays, and other tests. After weeks of living with a giant question mark over our heads, we finally had answers! To be completely honest, the first few days after being diagnosed, I was so scared. I had no idea what it was or what to expect. Pulmonary fibrosis scars and thickens lung tissue and affects your respiratory system. Healthcare providers consider pulmonary fibrosis a terminal illness. My mind always tends to think the worst. Searching my symptoms on the internet did not help ease any of my fears either! I'm sure you know what I mean – according to the medical websites you will be dead within the next few days.

I had so many questions. Being a missionary wife in the Philippines, the thought of being so far from family and western medicine was a bit frightening. You cannot help but wonder – what are we going to do now? What about my children and my husband? My husband does not know how to cook, so who is going to feed the kids? He can't clean either, so how are they going to survive without me? You know, all those really important questions that run through your head.

Well, maybe those were some of the crazier thoughts, but all jokes aside, I was terrified! Every time these thoughts would overwhelm my mind, I'd have a little talk with Jesus. Prayer can do so much for your heart, soul, and mind. (Philippians 4:6-7)

When I was going through this time, I would talk to Him often. All the noise in my mind would go away. It was just me and Jesus. You too can experience peace through your difficult situation. Whatever the outcome may be, trust that He is in control. My heart, soul and mind were at peace. I know that talking to Jesus had everything to do with it.(Psalm 62:5)

I remember talking to Jesus and saying, "Lord, if this is what You want for me and my family, I'm okay with it. You know what is best for us." (I Thessalonians 5:18). To this day, I still don't understand how my results came back normal. I believe it was God. I call it a miracle! My Jeremiah 33:3.

I like talking to Jesus throughout the day. The awesome thing is that He is there for me at any time, day or night. Would you consider having a little talk with Jesus when you feel overwhelmed with difficult circumstances? Would you have a little talk with Jesus when the noise of this world overwhelms you? Just pray and talk to Him, even when you feel like you cannot put into words everything that is on your mind. Whatever you may be going through, whether physically, emotionally, or spiritually, I encourage you to have a little talk with Jesus.

"Trust in him at all times; ye people, pour out your heart before him: God is a refuge for us. Selah." Psalm 62:8

prayer

Date: / /   Scripture:

Notes:

Requests:

Blessings:

Prayer Changes...Me!

By Kim Thompson

And the Lord turned the captivity of Job, when he prayed for his friends...
Job 42:10

"Prayer Changes Things" is a theme I have heard all my life. I can't even count the number of times I have seen a plaque, a magnet, or some form of decoration with these three words preaching the life-changing message. Prayer does change things, but I fear more often than not, a self-righteous spirit seduces us to believe that it's our neighbor who needs to change, but, oh no, not the wonderful "me"!

After living in three different countries, I have experienced that human nature is fairly the same anywhere one goes! There are happy church members, and there are unhappy church members. At one point in our ministry, we faced some of the latter kind, and that situation literally broke my heart until the night some of the disgruntled members decided to quietly mock their pastor (my husband) during the preaching. I sat two rows behind the ongoing drama. Anger instantly pulled my heart into a chokehold and held me captive. As the invitational hymn started playing, I raced down to the altar. I was going to give God an earful about these mean-spirited people and how they were being so unfair! As I started to pray that God would change them, something happened: the sweet, soft, gentle voice of the Holy Spirit told me to pray for them. What? Pray for them?! My mind submitted as my heart carried on in captivity. However, it didn't take long for the Lord to turn the captivity of my heart as I prayed for those members ... I arose from the altar a changed woman! I looked at those people with love in my heart! Prayer had changed me!

Does bitterness, jealousy, envy, pride, lust (you name the sin) hold you captive? If you want sweet release from your chains, prayer is the key that fits the lock to your prison cell. Prayer does change many things, but maybe most beneficial of all, it changes us!

prayer

Date: /   /   Scripture:

Notes:

Requests:

Blessings:

Praying for Her

By Nicole Redmon

I exhort therefore, that, first of all, supplications, prayers, and intercessions, and giving of thanks, be made for all men;

1 Timothy 2:1

One of the most precious persons in my life has been my pastor's wife. She has been such a blessing to me throughout the years. I treasure her dearly! I make it a point to pray for her every single day. Did you know that pastor's wives can be some of the loneliest folks? One would think that because of her position that she would have the most friends of all the ladies in her church. This simply is not true for most pastor's wives. She may be available, approachable and even show herself to be friendly, but that does not mean that she has those meaningful relationships where she feels secure to be her honest self. So, I pray for God to give her authentic friendships.

Satan has special targets made up for the pastor and his family. Satan wants to destroy your man of God and all that he loves, especially his wife and children. These bonds are strong. He will stop at nothing to destroy them. So, I pray for a hedge of protection around her.

The Bible does not list the qualifications for a pastor's wife. There are many qualities listed in His Word that we as women should strive to meet, but nothing is ever said about what is required of her. A very wise lady in the Lord once reminded me that her "job," if you will, as her pastor's wife, was to be his helpmeet! Why do we feel it necessary for her to teach the children's Sunday school class, keep the nursery, clean the church, decorate the sanctuary, have weekly Bible studies, and organize the next church potluck dinner? Your pastor's wife may do all these things and more, but only under her husband's direction. Please, do not put expectations on her that you truly would not place on yourself. So, I pray for her to know that her husband is her ministry and to serve in this area with loving creativity and to the best of her ability.

Her husband is always ready and willing to jump up at a minute's notice to minister to his flock. There may be a church family that needs counseling or comfort because they are burying a loved one (and that's just the first part of the week!) It would be very easy for envy to settle into the pastor's wife's heart. She may feel that she and the kids get the pastor's leftover time. Ministry is about people. And giving of his time is part of it. So, I pray against bitterness and resentment toward her husband being away at times and that the Lord will allow her to witness the miracles of seeing families put back together and folks being born again.

There are a hundred ways I could list how I pray for her. These are just a tiny bit of what her pages look like in my prayer journal. I'll leave you with one more way to pray. Pray for her devotional life. Pray that it is profitable and productive. We all need that special, private time with the Lord. So, I pray for her to have tender, precious moments with the Savior.

I challenge you this: ask her how you can pray for her and take the next thirty days to call her name out to God everyday. She is worth it, I promise!

prayer

Date: / /   Scripture:

Notes:

Requests:

Blessings:

Powerful Prayer

By Julie Payne

...The effectual fervent prayer of a righteous man availeth much.

James 5:16

I am just in awe of how God keeps us safe in situations that we do not even realize what could have happened. When I meditate on this, I can't help but wonder how many dangers are kept from people I love because of prayers that have gone up on their behalf!

Prayer – While it is the act of talking to God in the sense we are discussing, it has the specific meaning of "asking for a favor; particularly with earnestness." As it says in Hebrews 4:16, we, as children of God, have the access to come before Him, the Almighty God, in prayer; that is to ask a favor of Him! It is wonderful He wants this of us, who are just sinful flesh. To think that God hears the requests, cries, and burdens of our hearts, is just amazing!

Prayer and tears go hand in hand. David in Psalm 56:8, "...put thou my tears into thy bottle:..." Those tears the Lord bottled up is such a wonderful picture of Him hearing and remembering our requests, and our burdens! Those prayers with tears will be especially kept by our Great God, and will be as precious to Him as they are to us. So, don't ever feel like your prayers are not doing any good. Do not think "what's the use?" Be encouraged that God is faithful in His promise. Keep up those prayers, don't lose those burdens, and definitely don't feel discouraged!

Now, let's get to the part where God answers our prayers. Oh, what power! Isn't it a great encouragement to see God answer our prayers; to see the different ways He'll work to bring it to pass? What about those prayers He answers we don't even know about? As I mentioned earlier, it's wonderful to see God's Hand of protection, His answered prayer, when there's a "close call" involving a loved one – one that we had no time to pray about at the time, but the answer was a result of a past prayer – one He had in remembrance! Then my mind thinks – What has He answered that I have never seen? What dangers were kept from us by God's powerful interference? It's basically answered prayer that we never see – it boggles my mind and excites me at the same time!

Next time you are in a "close call," realize and rejoice that the powerful God kept His promise to hear and answer prayer! He answered someone's prayers for you. Keep those prayers up so that your prayer may be answered on someone else's behalf! Your prayers can make a difference. Thank you God for powerful prayer!

> To think that God hears the requests, cries, and burdens of our hearts, is just amazing!

prayer

Date: / /   Scripture:

Notes:

Requests:

Blessings:

Prayer for the Weary Mama

By Courtney Womack

Trust in him at all times; ye people, pour out your heart before him: God is a refuge for us. Selah.

Ps 62:8

Dishes are piled high, and you haven't brushed your hair, let alone your teeth since you got up. The baby is crying, and another kiddo can't find their shoes. You witness a wreck while taking the kids to school, causing more delays. It's a great morning, isn't it, Mama?

Often we let our days get so busy that we don't stop and talk to the Lord. Some seasons in life are more challenging than others, so we must work on our prayer life daily! A relationship will never grow if we don't communicate, and it also won't ever succeed if we constantly demand our wants! We must uplift one another, share our thoughts, and explain our needs. After much trial and error, here are a few ways I've been able to pour prayer into my daily life.

Pouring out of Thanksgiving (Phil. 4:6)

While washing those sky-high dishes, stop and give a prayer of thanksgiving to the Lord for those hungry, happy kids that keep filling your sink with dishes. Pray for the lady that would give their right arm to trade spots with you and have a family or loving husband. Call them out by name!

Pouring out for Today (Col. 4:2)

While on the way to drop the kids off, you saw that wreck! Why did it stop you in your tracks? Because you realized very quickly if that kiddo hadn't lost their shoes, that car accident could have been you! Thank the Lord for His protection; sit and ponder the blessings He has showered on you today! I have even begun to pray some of my thanksgiving and daily prayers aloud. Think about those little eyes and ears that are watching your every move. What will they do when you start openly and outwardly praising the Lord for His goodness and praying for daily strength, guidance, and grace? It will show your family/friends the importance of open thanksgiving to the Lord. It will also open a line of communication with Him that will become a habit!

Pouring out for Tomorrow

Now, you are taking a moment to sip that last sip of cold coffee before folding five loads of laundry. While mindlessly folding that laundry, pray for your family! When you pick up your hubby's dress shirts, pray for him to be the spiritual leader your home needs. How about his socks? Pray for him to be a witness in places he goes this week. Not to leave out the children - when you get to their clothes, pray for their future spouses, health or spiritual needs, and purity. It doesn't matter if they are two years old or twenty; they need your prayers!

You are aware of the needs of your family, your friends, and yourself. These are just a few examples of making it a daily habit to incorporate prayer into the little things during your day. Pouring out prayer daily to the Lord will change your life. You will never regret it!

prayer

Date: / /   Scripture:

Notes:

Requests:

Blessings:

In His Time

Anonymous

*I waited patiently for the LORD;
and he inclined unto me, and heard my cry.*

Psalms 40:1

We pray, we wait, asking and hoping
That God will hear and grant our desire.
But days turn to months, and months to years,
Is God even listening at all?
Then at once, He is there, in all of His glory,
Eyes clouded with tears, we see clearly His plan.
Faith is rewarded as the Scriptures have told us,
And the wait is always worth it all!

He gives us beauty for ashes, joy for mourning,
Instead of grieving, the garment of praise.
Always and ever, in His good time,
God will make all things beautiful.

- JBW

George Mueller once spoke of never letting yesterday's unanswered prayers keep us from praying in faith today. This has encouraged me many times when my own feelings were shouting for me to give up in prayer. Those moments when our faith seems weakest are when we need to trust and commit even more to seek the Lord and pray until He answers.

Charles Spurgeon said, "Delayed answers are not only trials of faith, but they give us an opportunity of honoring God by our steadfast confidence in Him under apparent repulses." David reminds us in the Psalms that he "waited patiently for the Lord; and he inclined unto me and heard my cry" (Psalm 40:1). Isaiah speaks of the Lord waiting on us, "And therefore will the Lord wait, that he may be gracious unto you..." (Isaiah 30:18a). Our God is sovereign, and His timing is always perfect.

Many are the moments in my life when I have begged the Lord to answer my prayers today and "right now." Looking back, I have been so grateful that He waited to grant those requests because He sees what we do not see. May we learn to appreciate the closeness we will share with the Lord as we patiently wait on Him in prayer.

"The problem with getting great things from God is being able to hold on for the last half hour." -Unknown

prayer

Date: / /   Scripture:

Notes:

Requests:

Blessings:

How Could I Pray For Hurtful People?

By Larissa Bell

*And this commandment have we from him,
That he who loveth God love his brother also.*

1 John 4:21

I cannot lie. It is not hard for me to pray for people who are nice to me. It is even easy for me to pray for people I do not know – broken down on the side of the road? In a fender bender? I got you! I pray for safety from injury, financial help to repair their car or replace it, wisdom in dealing with insurance companies, and so on. But praying for my enemies? People who hurt me or my family? That gets a little more challenging.

Sure, I could pray as David did a few times in Psalms when he asked God to destroy his enemies. However, I know from other Bible passages that this is not a Christlike response. I John is full of verses about loving others – including enemies and people who have hurt

Pray for God to reveal anything that needs changing or correcting in your life to help resolve the discord or disunity.

you. He even says that I cannot claim to love God if I don't pray for them. Then Jesus, Himself, taught about doing good to those who hurt you and despitefully use you. (Matthew 5:44, Luke 6:28)

More than likely, you have been hurt by people, even people who call themselves Christians and go to church. Just as the Pharisees were in the Bible, people are ready and willing to cast stones of judgment without grace, mercy, or love. God reminds me about Saul, a zealous, religious person in his day. He whole-heartedly believed persecutions of "blasphemers" were pleasing God. I am sure many Christians were praying for God to "take care of him" and ease their suffering. "But God." God got a hold of him and he, now Paul, turned his zealous efforts towards the spread of the true Gospel (Acts 9)!

Can you imagine how different our Bible and world would be without Paul's teachings? So, one way to pray for enemies that your flesh does not want to pray for is that God's will would be done in their life. His ways are higher than ours. We cannot see the big picture to know what their potential may be. We must try to remember that we are not the judge or jury. We are but dust, no better than they are, and have our own sins to pray about! Just take a look at Psalms 103:8-17. Is there pride? Are you basing your thoughts and judgements on truth and good things (Matthew 7:3-5, Philippians 4:8)? Pray for God to reveal anything that needs changing or correcting in your life to help resolve the discord or disunity.

My other frequent prayer is that the cause of Christ is not hurt or slandered by the situation. "Hurting people hurt people" is a well-known quote that reminds us that our flesh is prone to react and lash out when hurt. It is unfortunate that people fail to think ahead of the harm they are doing when they put their unfiltered feelings on Facebook, podcasts, blogs, or even gossip to others in the church. They fail to consider that many Christians and unsaved alike have been turned off to church and a relationship with Christ due to a Christian's or church's response to hurtful people. So, we should pray that people do not stray from the faith or fail to accept our perfect Christ because of imperfect Christians going through life's challenges.

Challenge: Write down a list of people or situations that are hurtful or hard to pray for. Take those names and burdens to God every day for the next week and ask Him to work His will in their lives. Ask Him to show you anything in your own life that may be complicating or contributing to the situation. Then pray that God will be glorified as He works "all things together for good."

prayer

Date: / /   Scripture:

Notes:

Requests:

Blessings:

We Ought Always To Pray

By Debra Birner

Be careful for nothing; but in every thing by prayer and supplication with thanksgiving let your requests be made known unto God.

Philippians 4:6

Have you gone to battle in prayer? Are you a prayer warrior? Wow – that doesn't sound so light and fluffy: battle, warrior.

Sometimes it's more like a struggle to start to pray. Prayerlessness is easy. Why is that? It's not that we don't have the Spirit of God in us, or that we don't know that it is His will for us to pray. After all, it's just talking to our Father about everything.

Matthew 26:41 - "Watch and pray, that ye enter not into temptation: the spirit indeed is willing, but the flesh is weak."

It is indeed a fleshly problem. My flesh is so weak. I am so easily distracted. This is why it is vital to remember that others need my prayers, that I need my prayers, that prayer does indeed change things.

But most importantly of all, my prayers are not foremost so that things can be changed, problems can be solved, souls can be saved. The main reason for my prayers is RELATIONSHIP. I love God. God loves me. He desires for me to spend time with Him.

Jeremiah 31:3 - "The Lord hath appeared of old unto me, saying, Yea, I have loved thee with an everlasting love: therefore with lovingkindness have I drawn thee."

So when I am distracted or busy or lazy ... I need to remember the One who created me in order to have a relationship with Him.

1 John 4:19 - "We love him, because he first loved us."

I never leave my prayer time wishing I had gotten something else accomplished.

The main reason for my prayers is RELATIONSHIP.

prayer

Date: /   /   Scripture:

Notes:

Requests:

Blessings:

Always to Pray

By Kaylena Cinereski

*And he spake a parable unto them to this end,
that men ought always to pray,
and not to faint;*

Luke 18:1

How often should I pray? The Bible says we are always to pray! I believe I fail to have a consistent prayer life as God desires. Instead of always praying, I find myself fainting in the area of prayer. I fail to remember that prayer is the direct way to have fellowship with my Father. But prayer also gives me power and strength! With little prayer, there is little power. With much prayer, there is much power. I want to have a powerful prayer life! God has given prayer to me for my benefit-to walk more closely to Him! Every single day, I should be in constant communication with God. It should feel odd to go hours without speaking to Him.

Prayer is so much more than just getting what I want. Prayer is a way for me to have a close-knit, daily relationship with my Savior. As a child of God, why on earth would I want to go through this life without that relationship? Speaking to Him, having fellowship with Him, and bringing my requests before Him are all benefits of prayer. I know if I ask anything according to His will He will hearken unto me (1 John 5:14). I know it is the will of God – that I come to Him in prayer.

A prayer-filled life can feel like a hard goal to achieve. But why? God could not have made it any easier for me to obtain! I believe I fail as a Christian to pray as much as I should, because I let the cares of this life become more important than prayer, rather than consistently being in prayer about this life! I fail to pray always.

I need to remember that God wants to have this fellowship and communication with me as His child. He wants to help me in every circumstance. God cares for me so much that He already knows my needs before I even ask! What an amazing thought! Matthew 6:8 says, "...for your Father knoweth what things ye need of, before ye ask him."

I have never been disappointed when I consistently have that fellowship in prayer with my Holy Father. My faith and closeness to Him grows, peace overcomes my heart, work begins in different areas of my life, and I see Him work in other's lives through intercessory prayer. Prayer will only help me grow in Christ and grow closer to Him! In fact, my growth in Him will be stunted if I fail to pray! When I begin to think I am good in my prayer life, I should pray even more. Remember "always to pray and not to faint."

prayer

Date: / /   Scripture:

Notes:

Requests:

Blessings:

Teach Us To Pray

By Elizabeth J. Garrett

And it came to pass, that, as he was praying in a certain place, when he ceased, one of his disciples said unto him, Lord, teach us to pray...

Luke 11:1

Recently, a visiting pastor at our church was preaching on prayer, and he made a comment on this verse that impacted me. Prayer was not something "new"; the Jewish people knew to pray. The Old Testament is full of examples of people praying to God. Yet, in this passage, the disciples approached Jesus when He finished praying with a request for Him to teach them to pray. There was something about Jesus' prayer that made an impression on them and caused them to desire to pray as He prayed.

What was it about Jesus' prayer? Why did Jesus even pray at all since He is God? Why would God need to pray to God? There are many possible answers, but there are two thoughts that I would like to share with you regarding Jesus' prayer. It is nothing new, but just a reminder for us.

First, Jesus prayed to have communion with His Father. The very term "Father" implies a special relationship. Jesus said in John 10:30,

"I and my Father are one." Jesus had limited Himself to a human body and was not present in Heaven with the Father. Therefore, He prayed to commune with God. How often does our prayer become mechanical? We know how to pray: we remember to thank the Lord for His blessings, to present our petitions, to intercede for others. But when was the last time you or I just communed with our Heavenly Father? Have you ever simply come into His presence and shared your thoughts and heart with Him and allowed Him to speak to you? In Genesis, we find that God descended to the Garden of Eden in the cool of the day to have communion with Adam and Eve. He desires for us to want to commune with Him and enjoy that special Father-child relationship with Him!

Secondly, Jesus prayed to show His dependence upon His heavenly Father. It is interesting throughout the Gospels, that Jesus prayed before every "big" step or decision in His life. For example, in Luke 6:12-13, Jesus went into a mountain and prayed all night. The following day, He chose His twelve disciples. In Luke 3:21, He was baptized and prayed. All four Gospels record that Jesus prayed in the Garden of Gethsemane before He was arrested and crucified. When we pray, we are expressing a dependence upon our Heavenly Father. We come to Him acknowledging that we cannot do anything on our own, but that we need Him to work on our behalf!

May this reminder refresh our prayer life and send us all to our prayer place!

prayer

Date: /   /   Scripture:

Notes:

Requests:

Blessings:

P-R-A-Y-E-R

By Kelly Byrley

And it shall come to pass, that before they call, I will answer; and while they are yet speaking, I will hear.

Isaiah 65:24

I love a good acrostic. The Lord gave me this one to remind me of some important areas to focus on during prayer.

P-Praise Him

We should desire to praise the Lord for His goodness and for Who He is. He is the sovereign God of the universe, Creator of all things, and Savior of the entire world! He loves us more than anything, so how can we help but praise Him? We should praise the Lord and have a spirit of thankfulness. Psalm 100:4 is a well-known verse that describes how we should approach our prayer time.

R-Reveal Sin

Sin is tricky. Sometimes, we think we are fine going about our day not really sinning too much. Then, we ask the Lord to reveal what we have done wrong, and He's suddenly shining His light

We need to pray for those who are in the spiritual battle.

down into our hearts exposing our sin. Proverbs 28:13 reminds us that we cannot prosper with unconfessed sin. Asking the Lord to reveal our sin allows us to confess it and get back in fellowship with Him. We cannot miss this! Unconfessed sin blocks the Lord from hearing our prayers. Isaiah 59:2 makes this very clear.

A-Armored Soldiers

We need to pray for those who are in the spiritual battle. This includes ourselves and our families, but expands to our pastor and his family, fellow ministry laborers, missionaries, other Christians, and so on. We need to pray for protection and encouragement. It has never been more apparent that we are in a spiritual battle. 1 Timothy 2:1, Job 42:10, and Ephesians 6:18 are some great verses about praying for others.

Y-Yucky Stuff

Sometimes, awful things happen to us and when they do, we can run to our Comforter. It is important for us to share these things with the Lord instead of immediately running to others. At times, we may find ourselves in such deep pain that we cannot even form the words to say, but Jesus can articulate for us and intervene to the Father on our behalf. I am so thankful for Romans 8:26-27!

E-Eternal Salvation

We need to earnestly pray for the unsaved people in our lives. We should also ask the Lord to provide us with opportunities throughout our day to be a witness. The Lord is the Scheduler of divine appointments, but if we are not asking for those opportunities, they may not happen. We should also be praying for the salvation of the millions of people around the globe who have never heard the name of Jesus. They need the opportunity to hear the Truth! See Romans 10:14.

R-Request Anything

Philippians 4:6 is probably the most quoted verse about bringing our requests to the Lord. These requests can be anything from the tiniest thing to the biggest thing. I love Isaiah 65:24. I have had the Lord provide what I was going to request before I even had a chance to ask. What a loving God we serve!

This was in no way an exhaustive list of everything we should include in our prayer time. We can dig deeper into any of these areas, and there are countless more we could add. I pray that this is helpful as a starting point for someone who may be struggling in this area.

prayer

Date: /   /   Scripture:

Notes:

Requests:

Blessings:

Paying the Price of Prayer

By Misty Wells

Let my prayer be set forth before thee as incense;
and the lifting up of my hands as the evening sacrifice.

Psalms 141:2

It was 2:00 in the morning. As I sat rocking our little boy, I wondered what was to come. Earlier that day, my husband and I took him to see a specialist about some concerns we were having. Micah, at thirteen months old, could not crawl or walk. Sitting up without assistance was very difficult for him, and he was falling behind others his age as a result of these delays. With a broken heart, I fell before the Lord. The unknown of our circumstance brought me to a place of fervent prayer.

Micah would go on to see several other doctors and therapists. He would endure countless scans and blood tests and with all my being I wanted to take his place. During these days of great emotional cost, my prayer life was somehow stronger than it had ever been. This was one of the loneliest valleys I had walked through. Yet, the reality of a caring Heavenly Father was ever present! Mark chapter 4 tells us that Jesus began to teach the multitude by way of parables. During this great gathering, no doubt, lives were changed and many began to follow Christ. Verse 34 says, "... and when they were alone, he expounded all things to his disciples." Sometimes, loneliness is necessary in the prayer life of the believer. A ladies' conference will never sustain your relationship with God. He has much to expound to us if we will come before Him in the aloneness of prayer.

Our son walked up to me this morning, and I couldn't help but remember those days and nights spent bringing my petition before the Lord, drawing closer to Him with every sacrificial prayer. You see, it wasn't that God allowed our son to walk that so strengthened my faith. It was my seeking and His expounding that made me trust Him no matter the outcome. Some of the sweetest meetings with my Lord are those derived from a heart of sacrifice. Times where He is put in His rightful place...above all.

Dear sister, will you give your burden to the God of all comfort? Will you awake early? Momma, will you give that nap time to the Lord? Will you pay the price of prayer? Your Heavenly Father longs to commune with you. The benefits of being in the presence of One so precious far outweigh the cost.

prayer

Date: / /   Scripture:

Notes:

Requests:

Blessings:

Abiding in Prayer

By Coretta Gomes

But thou, when thou prayest, enter into thy closet, and when thou hast shut thy door, pray to thy Father which is in secret; and thy Father which seeth in secret shall reward thee openly.

Matthew 6:6

Prayer is one of the most important parts of our Christian walk, yet we pray so little compared to how much we should be praying. I too am guilty of this.

We take for granted that God will supply all our needs because we are His children. He so graciously does, of course, however, we let the business of our lives take over our days and forget to devote time in prayer. We might say a quick prayer here and there, but do we really take time out of our day to spend with the Lord in prayer?

The Bible tells us to "Pray without ceasing" in I Thessalonians 5:17. This means praying while washing the dishes, cleaning, folding clothes and the list goes on and on. But, He also wants us to abide in prayer. (John 15:7). Our Father wants to hear our petitions and concerns, to hear us share our burdens with Him, and to abide in Him in prayer!

God promises that when we abide in Him, He will abide in us. I have noticed throughout my life that when I do not take the time to abide in prayer like I should that my day does not go as smoothly. I do not get all that I need to do accomplished. On the other hand, on the days that I take more time to spend in prayer, my days flow more smoothly, and I can feel God's touch even in the small things. Not to say that we will not have rough days! We all have those days! But short-cutting our prayer life does not pay off! We are quick to fall on our knees and pray when things get tough, a loved one is sick or our world gets turned upside down.

We are so quick to forget to devote time in prayer when things are going well. The Lord is concerned with our small needs as well as our big ones. Jeremiah 33:3, "Call unto me, and I will answer thee, and shew thee great and mighty things, which thou knowest not." Are we, as God's children, seeing the "great and mighty things" we could be if we were devoting our time in prayer? Are we, our family, and church family missing out on blessings of the Lord because we are failing in the area of prayer? I would dare say that we have missed out on blessings and will continue to miss out on seeing what God can do for us and others because of our lack of abiding in Him in prayer.

How many times have we heard, "Oh my granny was such a prayer warrior. If anyone could get a hold of God, it was her." I understand that Granny might have had more time to pray, even so, that does not excuse any of us at any age from getting in our prayer closet and abiding in the Lord in prayer. We live in an uncertain, crazy world, and the Lord's coming is imminent. Are we praying for the Lord to save our lost loved ones as we should? Do we ask the Lord to guide our children in the right path and teach them the importance of prayer? Do we really pray for others when they ask us to or do we just say we will pray and then forget?

I want my children and others around me to see the "great and mighty things" He has in store for us. I would hate to miss out on what God can do for me because of my lack of prayer. Let us, as God's children, strive to "abide in Him." "Be careful for nothing; but in every thing by prayer and supplication with thanksgiving let your requests be made known unto God." Philippians 4:6).

prayer

Date: /   /   Scripture:

Notes:

Requests:

Blessings:

Praying for Your Friends

By Callie Payne

"...and pray one for another, that ye may be healed..."

James 5:16

How refreshing is it when you are going about your normal routine and you get that text-"You were on my heart today, and I prayed for you." Or you come into the midweek service with an unspoken request, and a friend nearby asks how to help you pray. It's nice being remembered in prayer, but how many times are we that praying friend to those around us?

How many people will you come in contact with today that are feeling weighed down with struggles in their world? Some people wear it on their gloomy countenance like their favorite t-shirt for all to see. But some hide it behind their smile. Are we taking the time to selflessly look up from our world long enough to notice those friends around us needing our prayer?

A prayer for your burdened pastor's wife may be just what gets her through a tough day; just as a prayer for a grieving widow may encourage her in a dark time. Your friends are counting on your prayers, maybe without even realizing they are. Rather than looking at your friends through selfish or critical eyes, be the friend that is looking through eyes to look for ways to better pray for them. Listen, share, and pray fervently for those around you. The verse says, "...the effectual fervent prayer of a righteous man availeth much."

Your friendships will only get stronger when you are bringing their needs before God. In Job 42, Job not only prayed for his friends, but he prayed for those trying to hurt him when they could not get a prayer through. In return, he was blessed abundantly. The Lord turned his captivity when he prayed (Job 42:10-12).

James says, "...and pray one for another, that ye may be healed..." Maybe the burdens you are bearing could be turned into a blessing if you began to pray on behalf of those friends counting on you. Even those that may be trying to hurt you.

Today's challenge: Make a list of the first four friends that come to your mind. Under their names, make bullet points of things you know they need help praying for in their life. You do not always have to tell them you called their name in prayer, but if you think it may be an encouragement to them, be a blessing to someone else today. And who knows, you may be the one to receive an even bigger blessing in return.

> A prayer for your burdened pastor's wife may be just what gets her through a tough day...

prayer

Date: /   /   Scripture:

Notes:

Requests:

Blessings:

The Hour of Prayer

By Dixie Sasser

Now Peter and John went up together into the temple at the hour of prayer, being the ninth hour.

Acts 3:1

The Western Wall, or Wailing Wall, in Jerusalem is one of the most sacred sites in all of Israel. The site is a relatively small section of a larger retaining wall of Herod's Temple which stood in the days of Jesus. The Temple itself was destroyed by the Romans in 70 AD. Today the Jews are not allowed to go up on the Temple Mount, the site where the Temple once stood, because the Temple Mount is under the control of the Muslims; therefore, they pray at the Western Wall because it is the closest they can get to the spot where the Holy of Holies would have stood.

The site is divided into a men's section and a women's section. There is almost always someone there praying, and at times the crowds are so large it is almost impossible to touch the Wall. Many will spend hours there praying. It is an amazing place to visit, yet a sad place.

Why? Because for all their devotion to times of prayer, God does not hear them. They do not have the Lord Jesus as their Savior, and it is only through Him that we have access to God (John 14:6).

What a wonderful thing to know that as a Christian, we have access to the Lord, and He hears our prayers (I John 5:14-15). Oh, but how sad to see how little we take advantage of this privilege. The Jews pray at least three times a day, and the Muslims pray at least five times a day; prayers that are vain and without answers. Acts 3:1 talks about the hour of prayer. How have we gotten so busy in our lives that even saying a blessing before a meal has gotten too hard for us to do? God has given us so many promises about prayer in the Bible – that our prayers will be answered (Jeremiah 33:3), that our prayers will benefit others (James 5:16), that He will strengthen us when we pray (Psalm 10:17) – these are but a few – and yet we neglect one of the greatest privileges we have as Christians when we fail to make time in our day for prayer.

If we ever want to see real change in our world, we must make prayer a priority. God wants to commune with us, to hear from His children, and have sweet fellowship with us every day of our lives. Let us get back to our hour of prayer.

(You can go to the website www.thekotel.org to see a live stream of the Western Wall.

prayer

Date: / /   Scripture:

Notes:

Requests:

Blessings:

Faithful in Prayer

By Corli Hall

Praying always with all prayer and supplication in the Spirit, and watching thereunto with all perseverance and supplication for all saints;

Ephesians 6:18

Don't you love when God does a specific work in your heart and life? I experienced this not too long ago. In the weeks prior to a new year rolling around, I typically ask the Lord to show me an area in my life that I can improve upon, an area to commit to Him for growth and change. I am not suggesting that surrender and growth should be limited to once a year. In fact, we should pray like the Psalmist prayed in Psalm 139:23-24. However, instead of clinging to a list of temporary resolutions (even though I have some from time to time), I ask the Lord to show me something particular I can commit to Him for the next 365 days, something of eternal value.

In those weeks of seeking the Lord, He started to convict me about my prayer life. At times, it was the Holy Spirit gently and quietly tugging at my heart with conviction. Other times, it was my husband's voice as he announced that our church theme this year will be prayer! Then he informs me that one of the new classes at our Bible college will be on prayer. Then, he will also be preaching a series on prayer! Not to mention

"Things happen which would not happen without prayer. Let us not forget that."

- Elizabeth Elliot

that he happened to share a new book – "How To Pray"! What about getting an opportunity to write a devotional on the subject of prayer! Coincidence? No. I believe this was the Lord confirming what I knew He was wanting me to work on. He was already providing resources for me to grow.

We can always thank the Lord for His faithfulness! The question is: how faithful are we to the Lord? There is one channel of communication for us to reach our Heavenly Father: speaking to Him through prayer. Do we pray much? Do we pray at all? In Ephesians 6, the Bible tells us how often to pray: always! In 1 Thessalonians 5:16, we are admonished to pray without ceasing. There is a reason for the emphasis on the frequency of prayer found in Ephesians 6:12.

We have been in missions and ministry for nearly two decades and the longer we serve, the more this verse rings true! Friend, we simply cannot afford to live this Christian life in our own strength and from our own resources. Attempt? Yes. Succeed? No. R.A. Torrey said: "Prayer avails where everything else fails." We serve a living God whose attributes surpass the qualities and strength of the seemingly most capable human being. When we exercise a life of prayer, we tap into the power and strength of the One who reigns supreme. The One who made the promises. The One who sees them through.

Prayer is the method that God Himself appointed for us to obtain the Holy Spirit. I want to be filled with the Spirit! I want to be filled to overflowing, to touch the lives of the lost, the broken, the unlovable – also those whom I serve and those who serve beside me. I desire to be a godly wife and a virtuous mother. I beg God daily that the time I'm given on this earth will count for His glory! I realize, however, that the best version I will ever be is Jesus living and working through me. Am I abiding in Him through prayer? Does it show? Do others know?

I have to understand that lasting fruit grows from a heart in submission, a will in obedience, and a knee bent in prayer! A heart in submission recognizes that a life of prayer is not optional, it is crucial. A will in obedience agrees that we must never be too busy or distracted to obey the command to pray. A knee bent puts into action both the heart and will in the matter of prayer.

May the challenges and struggles in life not be the only things that press us to pray. May our prayers be to give and not just to receive. What do we give in prayer? We give praise to a God who is worthy of all honor and praise and glory. Praise reflects a heart of thanksgiving. Elizabeth Elliot put it so well: "For one who has made thanksgiving the habit of his life, the morning prayer will be, 'Lord, what will you give me today to offer back to you?'" We give to others through intercession. Spurgeon said: "No man can do me a truer kindness in this world than to pray for me." When God transforms us through prayer, we extend His goodness to others. When my life is filled with prayer, the fruit of the Spirit abounds and graces those around me.

"Things happen which would not happen without prayer. Let us not forget that." Elizabeth Elliot

prayer

Date: / /   Scripture:

Notes:

Requests:

Blessings:

First Things First

By Alyssa Schutt

Unto thee, O Lord, do I lift up my soul.
Psalm 25:1

What is the first thing you do when you wake up in the morning? Do you make a cup of coffee? Do you take a shower? Are you an early bird and rise like a Disney princess with a big stretch and boom ... just like that ... you're awake? Or are you like me and just sit in your bed for ten minutes with your blankets wrapped around you trying to muster the urge to get up and actually get ready? Whichever of these we may be, we all eventually get up and start our day.

Looking at this same analogy in the aspect of prayer, what is the first thing we pray about when we enter the throne room and speak with Jesus? Are we right into our prayer requests? Do we enter with praise? Or do we start with confession? None of these ways are essentially wrong to start a prayer, but in the first verse of Psalms 25, David lifts his soul to his Creator in the act of surrendering to start his prayer. Before he prays about anything going on in his life, he gives his soul to God. What a powerful way to start talking to God in the form of surrender.

Looking at this verse spoke to me and challenged me in prayer. As Christians, we must give our souls to God before we give any requests in our lives to Him. Although, yes, God wants us to make requests to Him, He wants our souls more than anything. The Creator of the universe wants me! He wants my struggles and my hurts. He wants my burdens. He wants my soul. The Lord needs our surrender to Him in order to place us in a position of blessing and in a position where our prayers can be answered in a way He sees fit. It is possible that we could lose our trust in God when we are not surrendered to Him in prayer.

"God, I lift up my soul to You today. I am surrendered to You and You alone. Help me to trust You with whatever happens in my life and use my life to further Your Kingdom for Your honor and glory. I love You, Jesus. Amen."

This is a short prayer I use in my life constantly. I want the Lord to use me for His glory, and I want to surrender everything to Him from the time I wake up until I rest. Trust in the Lord, and lift your soul to Him today.

prayer

Date: / /   Scripture:

Notes:

Requests:

Blessings:

The Direct Approach

By Marissa Patton

"In all thy ways acknowledge him, And he shall direct thy paths."
Proverbs 3:6

How many times have I felt defeated? How many times have I felt my strength wane after a commitment I made to "do better"? How often do I lose my cool after a decision to not lose my cool? I am a person who thoroughly enjoys listening to godly podcasts, reading helpful biblical resources, and seeking out good advice about all topics of marriage, ministry, and motherhood. But here is my main struggle. I will go days and days trying to implement a new child training technique. I will be so determined to change my attitude about a certain situation my husband and I have a difference of opinion about. I attempt to change my spirit to a lady in the church who I felt has wronged me or someone I love. Yet, I do not ask God first to change me.

That is the problem. I will try. I am determined. I attempt. At no point when I was convicted about an issue I must change did I take the time to ask God for help. I did not acknowledge Him in any of my "ways" as Proverbs 3:8 says. Instead of doing a patch job myself, this is what I should have done - "My voice shalt thou hear in the morning, O LORD; In the morning will I direct my prayer unto thee, and will look up"

Psalm 5:3. I think it is about time that we start directing our prayer unto Him so that He can start directing our path. Let's take the direct approach.

So the next time you hear a message that prompts you to make a life change. The next time you read a biblical resource that points you in a spiritual direction. When you see something in your life that needs to be fixed, stop. Direct a prayer to the Lord about it! And then watch Him direct you into a path that leads to peace and joy through Him. Watch Him bring about a change that He alone can bring in your life.

prayer

Date: /   /   Scripture:

Notes:

Requests:

Blessings:

Promptly Pray!

By Janette Young

...continuing instant in prayer;

Romans 12:12b

Many times, we pray about daily situations in our lives, simply trusting that God will handle them. Sometimes, when we know what is going on, we will even try to "help" God answer the prayer. But sometimes you do not know what is going on, and you hear God say, "Pray!"

No doubt this has happened to you. I am reminded of two incidents in my life when God used my prayers to shelter and protect those I love when I didn't know the circumstances.

When my daughter and son-in-law were missionaries in South Africa, it was an exciting yet scary time for me as a mother. When they first arrived in the country, they found a beautiful farmhouse complete with a caretaker that was included in the rent! It was inexpensive and perfect for the children to run and play. However, they were thirty minutes from town and did not have reliable communication available in that area. They were unable to phone or email us and let us know

When God prompts you to pray, don't hesitate!

they had settled in. As the days went on and we heard no news from them, my husband and I got such a heavy burden. We began to pray for them day and night. God would sometimes even wake us up in the night to pray for them. This went on for over a week.

Finally, we heard from them! They had decided to move into another house in the city so they could be close to the people they were working with. They had enjoyed living on the farm because everything seemed so "safe" away from the city. What we did not know was that while God was using us to pray for them for wisdom and safety, God was granting them just that. One day right before they moved, the caretaker showed them a deadly black mamba he had killed under the tree right where the children had just been playing. If they would have been bitten, they would never have made it to the hospital in time. They also learned that the farmers in that area were being targeted and massacred by gangs. Many times, it would be days before their deaths were discovered because of the distance from town and neighbors. God used our prayers to give wisdom and safety when we didn't even know what was happening.

Another example comes to mind of the time when they were flying home from South Africa. The eighteen-hour flight was going smoothly, and everyone was asleep. Suddenly, in the middle of the flight over the ocean, the plane started jolting and dropping. The turbulence was so rough that they were certain they were about to crash. The pilot even apologized later for the horrible turbulence. They didn't realize it at the time, but they were flying through the aftermath of Hurricane

Katrina that had just destroyed New Orleans. It had moved out into the Atlantic Ocean. They flew right into it. When they arrived home, they told us the story and said they truly thought they were going down that night. They told us that they had even made plans on who would sit beside the children and hold them if the plane started to crash. It was a very frightening story. My husband looked at them and asked, "What time did this happen?" When they told him, he and I looked at each other and started weeping. God had awakened us at that exact time to pray for them!

When God prompts you to pray, don't hesitate! He may be using you to be an answer to someone else's prayer! You may have to wait until you get to Heaven to find out just how God answered your prayer, but whatever you do – don't ever stop praying!

prayer

Date: / /   Scripture:

Notes:

Requests:

Blessings:

A Testimony of Prayer

By Ruth Weaver

...The effectual fervent prayer of a righteous man availeth much.

James 5:16

As a Christian, having a life of prayer should be a vital part of our life. Prayer is talking and spending time with God, whether on your knees, sitting in a chair or driving down the road. I Thessalonians 5:17 says "Pray without ceasing." (Note: While driving down the road, I recommend you use the verse I do, Mark 14:38 "Watch ye and pray..."). God loves for us to talk to Him each and every day in fervent prayer.

I am reminded of an occasion some weeks ago. While working around the house, I got a phone call from my dad. He informed me that my mom had fallen. Finding out that she was doing well and able to get up off the floor on her own was a relief. After the call ended, I started trying to figure out how my seventy-seven year old mom could get up on her own. Then, I remembered back when I was a child seeing my mom on her knees many times at the foot of her bed praying for us and others. Being so young, I didn't know how much her prayers meant to me and my family. But as an adult, it means the world. Because she was used to being on her knees, she was able to get herself up from her fall.

How is your prayer life? Will you have a testimony of being a prayer warrior? Can someone ask you to pray for them and you actually take the time to pray? I am trying to set a practice that when someone asks me to pray for them, I pray right away. No, you may not be able to get on your knees to pray, but God still hears you when you call. In Jeremiah 33:3 it says, "Call unto me, and I will answer thee and show thee great and mighty things which thou knowest not."

Talk to Him today. Ask Him to help you every day to desire Him more. Spend more time in effectual, fervent prayer. Our country, our church, our community, our world, and, most of all, our families need prayer. Will you have a testimony of having a fervent prayer life with the Lord?

prayer

Date: /   /   Scripture:

Notes:

Requests:

Blessings:

Getting God's Attention Through Prayer

By Nicky Schutt

"Out of the depths have I cried unto thee, O LORD."

Psalm 130:1

In 2019, a group of about fifty people (from our church and some from other churches) started a prayer group called "The Awakening Covenant." We fasted from food and all electronic devices every Monday for a year. I got to be part of that group, and it changed my life. My walk with God and prayer life has not been the same. What an experience! I started realizing I could truly get God's attention and experience the power of prayer that could change my life, our church, our community, a city, and even the world.

Listen to this quote: "Our prayers lay the track down to which God's power can come. Like a mighty locomotive, his power is irresistible, but it cannot reach us without the rails." God's power is always there and always available, but if it doesn't have a way to get to us it is to no avail. How does it get to us? God's power comes from being in God's presence and prayer. Prayer is what gets the attention of God, not our performance. Satan fights prayer in our lives but we must remember where our power comes from and that's why he fights it.

How can we pray so we can get the attention of God?

Pray honestly (Psalms 130:1-2) David is not pretending he is somewhere spectacular in life. He admits "out of the depths," or in despair. He is desperate. Be honest with God where you are spiritually. He already knows. Let's stop pretending we are something that we truly are not. Be real with God so He can be real to you.

Pray when you are hurting (James 5:13a) When you are sick physically, you go to the doctor. When you are sick spiritually, you go to God through prayer. He wants to help you.

Pray when you are feeling great (James 5:13b). Don't think because everything is going great, I shouldn't pray. Do daily "check ups" with God. Keep short accounts with God.

Pray when you are sick (James 5:14).

Pray when you have sinned and ask for a clean heart (James 5:15b-16). One of the hardest things to do is to swallow our pride and ask God to forgive us. However, it is the only way to keep that relationship connected the way it should be. There is nothing greater than a restored relationship with your Heavenly Father. Don't think you've gone too far away from God. Jesus paid it all and He wants to forgive it all.

My sister in Christ, I pray this devotional will be something that encourages you to begin having a fervent prayer life. Our families need praying moms, praying wives, praying sisters and on and on. Most of all, we need prayer to keep us disconnected from Satan and connected with Christ!

prayer

Date: / /   Scripture:

Notes:

Requests:

Blessings:

Call on The Name of The Lord

By Kate Ledbetter

Then called I upon the name of the LORD; O LORD, I beseech thee, deliver my soul.

Psalm 116:4

What a blessing to be given the gift of prayer! As I thought on this topic, the words, "call on the name of the Lord," are what came to my mind. It is such a privilege in every aspect and time of life to call on the Lord's name. In trouble, in heartache, in blessings, and in thanksgiving, we can simply include Him in recognition that He belongs in every part of this life He has given us. This desire to include the Lord will have you speaking to Him all day long as you, "Pray without ceasing" (I Thessalonians 5:17). You'll have a continual desire to call on His name.

Four times in Psalm 116 it speaks of calling on the name of The Lord. It gives us a picture of the Psalmist's desire to include the Lord in the differing aspects of a full life.

Verses 1 and 2 speak of calling on the Lord simply because you love Him for His listening ear.

Verses 3 and 4 speak of calling on the Lord to deliver us in times of death, trouble, and sorrow.

Verses 5 -13 speak of being thankful for the deliverance the Lord sends when we call, and in that salvation a desire to call on The Lord even more.

Verses 14-19 speaks of giving thanks when we come to Him in recognition of Who He is and how that leads us to want to call on Him more and more.

When you love the Lord and your desire is to cultivate a relationship with Him you'll find yourself, as the Psalmist, calling on Him, and calling on Him, and calling on Him more and more. As you call, you will find it becomes less and less about you and more and more about Him. In the end (verses 18 and 19) you'll be encouraging others to call on the Lord simply because He's so worthy to be praised!

prayer

Date: /   /   Scripture:

Notes:

Requests:

Blessings:

Is Sin Keeping You from Prayer?

By Grace Shiflett

And it came to pass, that, as he was praying in a certain place, when he ceased, one of his disciples said unto him, Lord, teach us to pray,...

Luke 11:1

In this verse, we see Jesus setting the example to pray. One of the disciples asked the Lord to teach them to pray. Interestingly, he didn't ask to be taught how to pray, but to pray. The longer I go in this Christian journey, the more I see the importance of prayer. Yes, we have all heard great messages about prayer or read books that stirred our souls with the desire and awareness of prayer. I wonder how many times we have been guilty of being "a hearer of the Word" and not "a doer" when it comes to prayer; being stirred but not changed. What good has it done if we have been challenged to pray but never actually pray? There are many excuses why a child of God may not pray, but I believe the main reason is sin in the life of a believer (Psalms 66:15).

You can sin and go to church, sing in choir, read your Bible, dress right, tithe, give to missions, and more. But you cannot sin and pray. So, do you pray? If not, then what is holding you back? If it is sin, then by all means confess and forsake it so you can know the wonderful blessing of prayer! Can I encourage you today to pray? Stop talking about it or making excuses and just pray. Have that special time with the Lord. Everyday stop what you are doing and pray. As a saved child of God, we have access to the God of heaven. What a wonderful privilege for the child of God! "... Lord, teach us to pray ...."

> So, do you pray?
> If not, then what is holding you back?

prayer

Date: / /   Scripture:

Notes:

Requests:

Blessings:

Teach Me to Pray

By Rikki Beth Poindexter

And it came to pass, that, as he was praying in a certain place, when he ceased, one of his disciples said unto him, Lord, teach us to pray, as John also taught his disciples.

Luke 11:1

I personally struggled with "prayer" as a young convert. The "how to" and "how long" was a bit overwhelming. I felt there was a right way and a wrong way. Even the disciples who walked with Jesus asked to be taught to pray. I remember as a young mother, reading two female authors that taught me so much about prayer. Two things specifically stood out: realizing how specific I could be and the organization of my requests. Prayer is our most powerful weapon as children of God! – I fear the one most neglected one.

We should desire a time to pray. Communing with our Lord is such a special, intimate time. We must make the decision to do it. Things will come up; distractions are real! We must be determined to pray. DO IT; set aside the time!! We will also have to defend our prayer time. Fight for that time each day!

We should desire a time to pray!

Realizing that I did not have to pray for everything and everyone everyday helped me so much! Being purposeful in making a prayer book has helped my daily prayer time in more ways than I could ever describe here. I moved away from a prayer list to a prayer book somewhere around 2013-2014. I would like to pass along some information that was helpful for me.

The model prayer in Matthew 6 teaches us to begin our prayer with worship and thankfulness. What if I have today only the things that I thanked the Lord for yesterday? What will I have? Am I a thankful person? I start my prayer time with being thankful. As the song says, "I've got so much to thank Him for!"

Maybe you are reading this, and you don't know where to start or would like to get more organized. I am going to give a website for a prayer notebook that can be purchased: ruthbumgardner.com

If you do not want to buy one on that website, get a small notebook, and divide it with tabs into "sections." Here are some of the "sections" in my personal prayer book: myself, my husband, my kids, extended family, friends, my pastor, church family/ministries, missionaries, enemies, pastor's wives, and other preachers. In each section I make the list or write the requests that need to be prayed over. Every section has its requests divided up into the days of the week. I take a few of the requests in each section and pray for them on Monday, a few for Tuesday, a few for Wednesday, and so on. I do this for every section in my prayer book.

For example, in my "church section," I have the names of every family in our church. I have those names divided into the days of the week. I am not praying for every family in my church, every day of the week. This way I can pray more specifically for a few families daily. Of course, I try to be sensitive, and pray over people and situations as the Lord burdens me.

I also have a "blessings section" or an "answered section." This is where I can keep up with all that the Lord is doing in my life and all of the prayers He is answering. If I come into a difficult or discouraging season in my life, I can look back at all that He has done for me! This section can help combat my doubt and worry.

I am hopeful that this little bit of information can help you as it did me several years ago. Feel free to reach out to me or the Highly Favoured Life team if I can be of more help.

Jas. 4:2 .....yet ye have not, because ye ask not.

prayer

Date: / /   Scripture:

Notes:

Requests:

Blessings:

About The Authors

Each author has been handpicked because of their testimony of Christ. God has gifted each writer with incredibly versatile perspectives of the Christian life. These godly ladies come from all walks of life including pastor's wives and daughters, missionary wives, church staff ladies, and faithful church members. Their written words of wisdom are sure to bless your heart.

To know more about our writers please visit:
thehighlyfavouredlife.com/about

Salvation Made Simple
By Renee Patton

Admit. One must first admit they are a sinner. Romans 3:10 states, "As it is written, There is none righteous, no, not one." Sin is everywhere and we all commit sin, many times without even trying. Perhaps in a conversation, we say something innocently, then realize it was not correct. That, my friend, is lying. Of course, murder is a sin that is seen and felt by those affected. However, lying is too. Jeremiah reminds one that "The heart is deceitful above all things, and desperately wicked: who can know it?" (17:9). A baby does not have to be told how to sin, it is simply in our nature. One must admit they are a sinner otherwise we make God a liar as found in I John 1:10, "If we say that we have not sinned, we make him a liar, and his word is not in us."

Believe. One must believe Jesus came to this earth to be born and die for our sins. "For God so loved the world, that he gave his only begotten Son, that whosoever believeth in him should not peish, but have everlasting life" (John 3:16). God desires that we should not perish, thus the choice is ours. God gives man the opportunity for salvation if man would take it. Romans 5:8 states "But God commendeth his love toward us, in that, while we were yet sinners, Christ died for us." Webster's 1828 Dictionary defines commendeth as entrusts or gives. So, God gave us His love through His Son, Jesus. Furthermore, Romans 5:19 shows how sin came from Adam and is made righteous through Christ, "For as by one man's disobedience [Adam] many were made sinners [mankind], so by the obedience of one [Jesus] shall many [mankind] be made righteous."

Confess. Confession is made with one's own mouth. The words must come from the person alone. Romans 10:9 talks of both confession and believing, "That if thou shalt confess with thy mouth the lord Jesus, and shalt believe in thine heart that God hath raised him from the dead, thou shalt be saved." The key is I have to confess to God. My husband or friend cannot confess for me. While God gives man the opportunity on earth, there will be a time every knee will bow and confess God is Lord, "For it is written, As I live, saith the Lord, every knee shall bow to me, and every tongue shall confess to God" (Romans 14:11).

To see more resources on salvation visit:
https://www.thehighlyfavouredlife.com/simple-salvation

If you made this decision, please contact us at *highlyfavouredlife @gmail.com*. We would love to rejoice with you in the new life you now have in Christ.

Highly Favoured Life Devotional Series

Buy on Amazon

www.ingramcontent.com/pod-product-compliance
Lightning Source LLC
Chambersburg PA
CBHW060324050426
42449CB00011B/2634